The Prodigal Daughter

by William Fry

Based on the Parable of The Prodigal Son

No performance of this play may be given without the written permission of the publisher to whom all applications for performing rights should be made, enclosing a reply paid envelope.

The performance time is approximately 30 minutes

Published by:
National Christian Education Council
Robert Denholm House
Nutfield
Redhill RH1 4HW

Published for:
RADIUS
Christ Church and Upton Chapel
Kennington Road
London SE1 7QP

British Library Cataloguing-In-Publication Data:
Fry, William
The prodigal daughter.
I. Title
822'.914
ISBN 0-7197-0668-8

A co-operative venture in Christian drama by NCEC and RADIUS

RADIUS is the shortened name of the Religious Drama Society of Great Britain, bringing together amateur and professional actors, writers, and others involved in religion and the performing arts.

RADIUS exists to encourage all drama which throws light on the human condition especially through a Christian understanding. It aims to help local congregations to a deeper appreciation of all types of drama, to inform them of opportunities to see work of a high quality, to give the technical advice and assistance needed for a good standard of local productions, and to help them find ways of introducing the lively arts into their worship.

The Society runs a unique lending library, organises an annual summer school, holds regular play-writing competitions and publishes its own magazine.

First published 1989 Reprinted 1989
© William Fry 1989

All rights reserved. No part of this publication may be reproduced, stored in a retrieval system, or transmitted in any form, electronic, mechanical, photocopying,recording, or other means without the prior permission of the publisher.

Reproduced and printed by Halstan & Co. Ltd., Amersham, Bucks., England

THE PRODIGAL DAUGHTER

PRODUCTION NOTES

This short play is intended for insertion in a normal Sunday service in place of the Bible readings and/or sermon. It is directly based on the Parable of the Prodigal Son (Luke 15.11-32) with the circumstances brought up to date but adhering as closely as possible to the story line.

Because of the perennial shortage of men, most of the characters in this version are women, though in some cases the sex can be changed if that is more convenient. The characters have all been given names, but it may be more effective if the performers use their own (e.g. the two daughters can use their own Christian names and the surname of the father) and if the name of their home-town is changed to the town or village where the play is being performed.

As the play is intended to be presented during the service, it should be performed without scenery or properties. The only things required are a table and three chairs. Although the stage directions describe complicated actions like cooking the breakfast and laying the table, these are simply intended to be mimed. However, if some properties are felt to be helpful, there is no reason why they should not be introduced.

The dialogue is intended to be entirely naturalistic, so the most important thing is that the performers should use the words that come most easily to them. Permission is hereby given for any minor changes to the script that may make the lines easier to say. The play lasts just over half an hour.

DRAMATIS PERSONÆ

in order of appearance

MOTHER	
FATHER	
KATHRYN	(their elder daughter)
TRACEY	(their younger daughter)
ELSIE	(the 'help')
CHARLENE	(Tracey's friend in London)
RITA	(a night-club manageress)
HARRY	(Rita's friend)
MRS GRIEVE	(an official of the DHSS)
JENNIFER	(Mrs Grieve's secretary)
ARTHUR	(a 'punter')

SCENE 1:

The Burgesses' kitchen/dining room

The scene opens at breakfast-time in the family home. A smallish table is set left stage centre and slightly at an angle with three chairs round it. Grumbling contentedly to herself, MOTHER comes into the kitchen to get breakfast for the family.

MOTHER Well, I don't know. Talk about Women's Lib! I wish I saw a bit more of it, that's all. First up every morning, five days a week; one wants this, another wants that. I suppose I should be grateful when their royal highnesses condescend to get out of bed. *(Going to the stairs and shouting up them)* Henry, do you know what the time is? It's nearly eight o'clock. Kathryn! Tracey! Where are you? Oh, why can't you get up in the mornings?

Enter FATHER. He gives his wife a practised and rather absent-minded kiss before sitting at table in the centre chair almost facing the audience. During the ensuing dialogue, MOTHER prepares the various breakfasts her family order and brings them to the table, but she herself never sits down.

FATHER Sorry, love.

MOTHER *(Still happily running through her customary list of grievances)* It's not for my sake, you know. I'm not the one who has to get off to work. Now, what are you going to have? How about a nice egg?

FATHER No thanks, love. Just the bacon and tomatoes.

MOTHER Why will you never have an egg? They're so good for you. *(Going to the stairs again)* Kathryn! Oh, there you are.

KATHRYN comes in with an air of quiet efficiency. She privately considers herself more mature than either of her parents, and in a sense she may be right. She kisses her mother and father with a perfunctory little peck.

KATHRYN All right, Mum. Don't fuss. I've got plenty of time.

MOTHER Not for a proper cooked breakfast, you haven't.

KATHRYN *(Sitting on FATHER's left with her back slightly turned to the audience)* Just give me some corn-flakes and a bit of toast.

MOTHER I wish you'd eat more... and where's Tracey? *(Going back to the stairs for a final shout)* Tracey, for the last time, breakfast!

Enter TRACEY, yawning loudly. As the younger daughter, she has long ago discovered that for her the best weapon is not behaving well but being cute.

TRACEY Hullo, Mum. *(Throws her arms round her neck to kiss her)* Hullo, Dad. *(Leans over him and rubs her face in his hair)* Morning, Kathryn.

TRACEY gives KATHRYN a wave as she sits down facing her on FATHER's right. KATHRYN has not been impressed by her greeting, but her FATHER and MOTHER are trying to suppress smiles of pleasure.

MOTHER Now, love, what are you going to have? Shall I scramble you an egg. The way you always like it?

TRACEY Oh, no thank you, Mum. Nothing but coffee.

MOTHER A little bit of toast?

TRACEY Just the coffee, thanks.

MOTHER *(Tutting sadly to herself as she goes back to the cooker)* Oh dear!

FATHER Tracey, what time did you get in last night?

TRACEY Oh, I don't know; a bit after midnight.

KATHRYN I'll say. You woke me at half-past two, slamming the front door.

MOTHER Tracey, love, I don't like you staying out as late as that.

TRACEY Come off it, Mum. I am eighteen.

FATHER It's no wonder you can't get up in the morning.

TRACEY What is there to get up for? I've left school. I haven't got a job.

FATHER You could go out and look for one.

TRACEY It's no good looking. There aren't any round here.

FATHER Kathryn didn't seem to have any trouble.

TRACEY That's different. She's got qualifications. Besides, there was more work to be had then. I'll never get a job in this dump.

MOTHER Now, don't talk like that. Here's your coffee.

TRACEY Of course it would be different in London.

FATHER That's as may be.

MOTHER *(Alarmed)* What was that about London?

TRACEY Nothing. I was only saying there were plenty of jobs there.

FATHER You don't know anything about it.

TRACEY Yes, I do. I've got friends in London and they've told me a lot.

KATHRYN What friends have you got in London?

TRACEY Charlene, for one.

FATHER I don't remember Charlene.

KATHRYN I do.

It is evident that she remembers no good of CHARLENE.

TRACEY She's got a good job in London and a flat and everything; and, what's more, she said I could stay with her if I came.

MOTHER *(Really frightened)* Henry, you're never going to let Tracey go up to London all by herself?

TRACEY I wouldn't be by myself. I told you - I could stay with Charlene.

MOTHER That's not the point.

FATHER Don't worry, love. She's not going on my money, I can tell you.

TRACEY It doesn't matter. I'm not asking for your money. I've got my own.

This thunderbolt leads to a short silence.

FATHER What do you mean, Tracey?

TRACEY You know: The money Gran left me. I can use that.

MOTHER That thousand pounds? You can't touch that. Gran left that to you for your future.

TRACEY Well, this is my future. If I use that money to go to London, then I can get a job. That's what Gran would have wanted, isn't it?

MOTHER A thousand pounds is a lot of money for a young girl. Your dad is looking after that for you, for your own good.

TRACEY *(Going behind FATHER's chair and winding herself lovingly all over him)* Dad, why can't I have my own money? After all, I am eighteen. I'm grown-up now.

This is only too true, and she is using all her feminine charms to get round him. Grim-faced, KATHRYN watches them, but their MOTHER is too worried to care.

FATHER Look, love, you know I only want to do what's best for you. As your mother says, it's a lot of money.

TRACEY Why shouldn't I have it? Kathryn's got her thousand.

FATHER Yes, and look what she's done with it. She's put it in a building society, and it gives her a little extra every month.

KATHRYN Yes, and I'm saving that as well.

MOTHER You see, Kathryn's the sensible one. Why can't you be like her?

TRACEY That's fine. She's got a job. She can afford to save her money. But I haven't. I've got to use mine to get a start in life.

MOTHER *(Coming over to TRACEY and putting an arm round her)* And besides, love, think how we'd miss you. The house wouldn't be the same.

FATHER *(Patting her hand)* That's true, you know, Tracey. We'd hate to lose you.

The sight of both her parents fondling her sister at once has its effect on KATHRYN. So far she has simply been irritated at watching TRACEY get her own way as usual, but suddenly it strikes her that there may be something in this for herself. After a pause, she speaks to her FATHER very slowly and reasonably.

KATHRYN You know, Dad, I think Tracey has got a point. After all, she's over age, and she does have a right to her own money.

FATHER *(Still holding TRACEY's hand)* Nobody's trying to take it away from her, Kathryn. We just don't want her to waste it.

MOTHER *(Cuddling TRACEY even more warmly than before)* She may be over age, but she's still an awful baby.

KATHRYN All right, but that doesn't alter the facts. If you don't give it to her, strictly speaking, she could take you to law.

MOTHER Is that true, Henry?

FATHER Tracey would never do a thing like that.

KATHRYN No, of course not; she's too nice. But do you want to take advantage of her good nature?

TRACEY *(Who cannot remember when she last heard such a loving speech from her sister)* Thanks, Kathy! That's really nice of you.

She runs to KATHRYN to kiss her, but KATHRYN, sho has a low opinion of these displays of affection, only shrugs and ducks.

KATHRYN No, I only want Dad to do what's fair, that's all. Anyway, I must be going.

She rises and makes for the front door.

MOTHER *(Taken aback by this sudden change of sides)* It isn't a question of being fair, Kathryn. Look, you've got a good head on your shoulders. Do you honestly think it would be good for Tracey to take all that money up to London?

KATHRYN Well, I don't know. It might help her to grow up a bit.

Exit KATHRYN by the front door.

TRACEY There you are! Even Kathryn thinks I ought to have it, and you know how she's always down on me.

MOTHER You're not going to give in to her, are you, Henry?

FATHER Well, love, you heard what Kathryn said. I don't know that we've got the right to keep it from her.

TRACEY *(Scenting victory)* Don't worry, Dad. I wouldn't take you to law. I know you'll do the right thing.

She turns away, leaving FATHER and MOTHER looking unhappily at one another.

FATHER *(To MOTHER)* We've really got no choice, love. She'll have to have it, if she wants it.

MOTHER Tracey, do you really want to go all that way?

TRACEY *(Still not looking at them)* It doesn't matter what I want, Mum. I'll do whatever you say.

This is too much for them. MOTHER looks back to FATHER and slowly nods her surrender.

FATHER Very well, Tracey. You can have the money.

TRACEY turns and dashes into his arms.

TRACEY Dad, that's so sweet of you. And you too, Mum. You'll never regret it, I promise you.

FATHER I'll call in at the bank this morning and tell them to take it off deposit. Then we can pay it into your account this day week.

TRACEY Next week! Can't I have it now?

FATHER You lose some interest if you don't give them notice.

TRACEY How much?

FATHER It'd be a bit under a pound, I think.

TRACEY A pound! But that's nothing. Come on, Dad, let's get it out this morning.

FATHER *(Laughing in spite of himself)* All right, you win. Come down to the bank at twelve, and I'll make the arrangements. *(Then, seeing the expression on his wife's face)* Look at the time! I must go.

As he reaches the front door, the doorbell rings. He opens it, and there is ELSIE standing outside. (The simplest way of achieving this is for ELSIE to hold up one finger, as if pressing a bell, and say 'Ding-dong!'

ELSIE Morning, Mr Burgess.

FATHER *(Who does not really like her very much)* Oh, hullo, Elsie. Nice to see you. I'm just on my way out.

Exit FATHER, thankfully. ELSIE comes in and starts taking off her coat.

ELSIE Morning, Mrs Burgess. Hullo, Tracey.

TRACEY Elsie, do you know what's happened? I'm going to get the money my Gran left me. We're going to the bank for it today.

ELSIE Ooh, that's nice. How much will that be, then?

TRACEY A thousand pounds.

This confirms everything ELSIE has always thought about the younger generation, but she struggles to keep a genial front.

ELSIE A thousand pounds! Well I never! And at your age, too! I wish someone would give me a thousand pounds, that's all I can say.

MOTHER is rather embarrassed that TRACEY has come out with all this to the 'help'. It does not bode well the future, nor will it make ELSIE any easier this morning.

MOTHER We haven't given it to her, you know. It's her own money. She's just collecting it today.

ELSIE Well, now! And what are you going to do with it?

TRACEY I'm going up to London.

ELSIE Oh! Going to have a gay old time, are we?

MOTHER No, of course not. She's going to get a job.

ELSIE That's difficult, these days.

TRACEY Not in London. There are lots of jobs there.

MOTHER *(Who is not much enjoying this conversation)* Now, Elsie, do you think you could hoover the bedrooms this morning?

ELSIE Oh no, Mrs Burgess, not with my back. My husband would never allow it.

MOTHER Well, what about doing out the kitchen?

ELSIE No, I don't think so.

MOTHER Then I don't know what to suggest.

ELSIE I tell you what. If you'll just get this table cleared, I'll settle down and polish the silver.

Exit ELSIE, presumably to take off her coat and put on her overall. MOTHER sighs and obediently starts clearing the table. TRACEY grins ruefully.

TRACEY Isn't she a marvel! Well, I must pack.

MOTHER *(Startled)* Why? What's the hurry?

TRACEY I haven't got long. The London bus goes at 1.15.

MOTHER You're not going today?

TRACEY What's the point in staying? Can I borrow your blue suitcase?

TRACEY makes off in the direction of her bedroom.

MOTHER Here, wait a minute! Let me come and help you. Have you got all your clothes clean? If only I'd known, we could have gone down to the shops and got you some really warm vests...

Chasing after TRACEY, MOTHER disappears from view, but her voice can still be heard, slowly dying away.

END OF SCENE 1

SCENE 2:

Charlene's flat in London

Enter CHARLENE, not looking at her best. She has only just got out of bed, her head aches, and her mouth tastes foul. She is wearing high-heeled mules, badly trodden over, and a dressing-gown intended strictly for private use. Making her way to the table (now a dressing-table) she looks with distaste at her own reflection in the mirror, reaches for her cosmetics and wearily begins on the repair work.

At this moment, TRACEY rings the bell of her flat. Unlike the ding-dong of the Burgesses, this gives a sinister little buzz. Surprised to have a visitor at this early hour, CHARLENE staggers to the door and opens it.

TRACEY Hullo!

CHARLENE *(Puzzled)* Hullo...

TRACEY Charlene, it's me - Tracey.

CHARLENE Oh, hullo. What are you doing here?

TRACEY I've come to stay.

CHARLENE Who with?

TRACEY You. Don't you remember? You said I could, any time I was in town.

CHARLENE Did I?

TRACEY Yes, you did. So I've come, and I've brought my case.

CHARLENE So you have. Well, you'd better come in.

Unwillingly, she backs into the room. TRACEY follows her, too excited to notice that she is not entirely welcome.

TRACEY *(Gazing round in delight)* It must be wonderful to have your own flat.

CHARLENE Yes, it's all right, but I not going to stay here. I'm going to get a place up the West End. Want a coffee?

TRACEY Thanks.

CHARLENE Make it, will you? You'll find everything over there.

She points vaguely in the direction of the cooker and sink. TRACEY trots over to oblige.

TRACEY Got a kettle?

CHARLENE Use the saucepan.

TRACEY It isn't very clean.

CHARLENE Oh, for pity's sake, you sound just like your mum.

TRACEY I can't turn the tap.

CHARLENE No, it's a trick. You have to hit it sideways.

TRACEY hits it sideways and it gushes down, splashing her clothes.

TRACEY *(Momentarily dismayed, but trying to look on the bright side)* It's nice and strong when it does come, anyway. Got any matches?

CHARLENE *(Throwing her a box)* Here you are.

TRACEY Thanks.

She lights the gas, which explodes with a loud pop. TRACEY gives a little scream. This makes CHARLENE start, and she accidentally smears lipstick across her cheek.

CHARLENE *(Wiping off the lipstick)* Ooh, you are jumpy, aren't you?

TRACEY Sorry! Got any coffee?

CHARLENE It's on the shelf.

TRACEY *(Finding it)* Oh, yes. Spoon?

CHARLENE Try the drawer.

The drawer resists TRACEY's efforts to open it and then suddenly gives way with a jerk, almost spilling on to the floor. TRACEY discovers a teaspoon and wipes it furtively on her sleeve before digging into the jar of instant coffee.

TRACEY The coffee's gone hard.

CHARLENE *(Losing patience)* Well, dig it out, then.

TRACEY digs it out with difficulty and is about to ask for cups when she notices two dirty mugs on the draining board. She looks into them with distaste, runs them under the tap, feebly tries to shake them dry, puts a lumpy spoonful of coffee into each and pours on the boiling water.

TRACEY Any milk?

CHARLENE *(With an air of superiority)* Milk? In London, everybody drinks it black.

TRACEY Oh... Sugar?

CHARLENE Sugar! Don't you care at all about your figure?

TRACEY Yes, I see.

She brings the two mugs over to the dressing-table, sits stage right of CHARLENE, who is now applying a heavy coating of mascara, and watches her with uncritical admiration.

CHARLENE Of course, when you're in the glamour business like me, you have to take care of yourself.

TRACEY What do you do, exactly?

CHARLENE Me? I work at a club.

TRACEY *(Impressed)* You mean a night-club?

CHARLENE Yes, you could call it that.

TRACEY Is it a famous one? What's it called?

CHARLENE Well, it's not famous exactly, but it's known in the right circles. It's called Eve's Apple.

TRACEY Oh! That's a nice name!

CHARLENE Yes, isn't it?

TRACEY And what do you do there?

CHARLENE I'm a hostess.

TRACEY What do you have to do? Dance with the customers?

CHARLENE That sort of thing. There's not much room for dancing, actually. It's more of an intimate atmosphere.

TRACEY What time do you start?

CHARLENE Ten o'clock.

TRACEY *(Dazzled)* At night? When do you finish?

CHARLENE It depends.

TRACEY Do you think I could get a job like that?

CHARLENE Well, I don't know. You need style for that sort of thing; you know - sophistication.

TRACEY *(Crestfallen)* Oh, I see.

CHARLENE Are you looking for a job, then? Is that why you've come?

TRACEY Yes. I couldn't get anything at Pendwick, so when I got Gran's money, I thought I'd try my luck in London.

CHARLENE *(On the alert)* Gran's money, eh? How much is it?

TRACEY A thousand pounds.

CHARLENE Oh! That's handy. That should last you till you get a job anyway. Have you got a bank account here?

TRACEY No, do you think I should have? At the moment it's all in cash.

CHARLENE Is it? Better look after it carefully.

TRACEY Oh yes, I'm carrying it on me.

CHARLENE Very wise. All right. You can stay here if you want to. Would you like me to see if I can get you something at the club?

TRACEY *(Thrilled)* Do you mean it?

CHARLENE I'll ask Rita. I don't suppose it'll be anything much to begin with. You know - start at the bottom.

TRACEY I don't mind what I do.

CHARLENE Good. That'll be a help. We'll have to dress you up, though. You can't go looking like that. Do you want to borrow one of my dresses?

TRACEY Can I?

CHARLENE Come on, and, while we're at it, we'll try to do something about your hair.

CHARLENE downs the rest of her coffee and leads the way into the bedroom with TRACEY scuttling excitedly after her.

END OF SCENE 2

SCENE 3:

Eve's Apple

As you have probably guessed, Eve's Apple is a nasty, disreputable club, which takes a great deal of money off its exclusively male clientele while offering as little as possible in return. It succeeds in attracting the would-be vicious and at the same time fending off the police by hinting at nameless debaucheries which never actually occur.

If you have a superfluity of young girls, here is a splendid opportunity to use them in group work to build up the atmosphere of the place. They might be leaning provocatively against doorposts, giggling in corners or jigging to music which you may or may not choose to let the audience hear.

However, they can just as well be imagined. The only essential characters are RITA, the manageress, and HARRY, her sole male employee. HARRY comes out through the door of the club and looks up and down the street. He calls over his shoulder to RITA.

HARRY Ready to open up, Rita?

RITA *(Emerging after him)* Might as well. Anyone about?

HARRY Not a soul. Don't worry. They'll be along.

RITA Tsk! If you had to pay the bills on this club -

HARRY Yeah, I wouldn't mind it, so long as I could have the takings.

RITA There's no money in it at all.

HARRY Come on! At the price you charge for drinks! *(Turning his head like a hunting beast of prey)* There's somebody coming now.

RITA No, it's only Charlene.

Enter CHARLENE and TRACEY, both dressed in the gaudiest frocks in CHARLENE'S wardrobe.

CHARLENE Evening, Rita. Evening, Harry.

RITA Who've you got there, Charlene?

CHARLENE Rita, I want you to meet a very particular friend of mine. Her name's Tracey.

RITA Oh yes?

CHARLENE She's come up to London to look for a job, and I told her I was sure you'd be interested.

RITA Sorry. I've got more girls than I can handle just at present.

CHARLENE That's all right. She can afford to wait. She's come into some money.

Imperceptibly, HARRY and RITA stiffen with interest.

RITA How nice! *(To TRACEY)* Large sum of money, would it be?

TRACEY *(Anxious to please)* A thousand pounds.

RITA *(Ostentatiously bored)* Oh, fancy! Well, you needn't think you can buy your way in here with your thousand pounds.

TRACEY Oh, no! I only wanted a job.

RITA What do you think, Harry? Could we use her?

Smiling, HARRY takes TRACEY by the chin, looking her over like a dealer buying a horse.

HARRY Well, I don't know. We might make something of her. Where do you come from, Tracey?

TRACEY Pendwick.

HARRY Yeah, I can imagine. Dead, eh?

TRACEY That's right.

HARRY You'll find life very different here. Do you think you can handle it?

TRACEY I'll do my best.

HARRY That's a good girl. You know, Rita, I think we ought to give this little lady a try.

RITA All right. If you say so.

HARRY Come on, Tracey, and see how you like it inside.

They pass out of sight.

CHARLENE Rita!

RITA Yes?

CHARLENE Don't you forget: I was the one who found her.

RITA All right, Charlene. You don't have to talk like that. You'll get your bit when the time comes.

Exeunt, whispering to one another.

END OF SCENE 3

SCENE 4:

At the Department of Health and Social Security

MRS GRIEVE comes in and sits down at the table in the upstage left chair. She is a pleasant, kindly, middle-aged woman, but continual contact with the failures of society has given her a slightly formidable manner. She heaves a little sigh and rings a bell on her desk. (Press on the desk with a finger and say 'Ding!')

Enter JENNIFER, her secretary, who is a very different personality. Disappointed in her own life and sickened by what seems to her the perpetual sponging of the irresponsible, she draws comfort from humiliating the applicants. She is particularly successful with newcomers, who have not yet armed themselves against her, and TRACEY will be easy meat for her.

GRIEVE *(gently)* Good morning, Jennifer.

JENNIFER *(Like a sergeant-major)* Morning, Mrs Grieve.

GRIEVE *(Sadly registering this tiny rejection of friendship)* Well, we'd better get started. Who's first this morning?

JENNIFER *(Consulting a list)* A young woman calling herself Tracey Burgess.

GRIEVE What's the name on her Insurance Card?

JENNIFER She hasn't got one.

GRIEVE I see. Would you ask her to come in, please?

JENNIFER Very well. *(Going to the door and calling)* Burgess!

TRACEY comes in, slightly scared.

TRACEY Is that me?

JENNIFER *(With a jerk of her head)* Over there.

TRACEY walks to the desk as if it were the execution block.

GRIEVE *(Very politely, perhaps to make up for JENNIFER's behaviour, but without apparent warmth)* Miss Burgess? *(TRACEY nods)* Do sit down. *(TRACEY sits in the chair downstage right of her)* Thank you, Jennifer. I'll call you as soon as we're ready for the next applicant.

JENNIFER Very good, Mrs Grieve.

She stalks out, clattering her high heels dangerously.

GRIEVE Now, Miss Burgess, what can we do for you?

TRACEY I need some money.

GRIEVE Oh, do you? Well, we're not a bank, you know. This is the D H S S, and we don't just hand out money to everyone who asks for it. *(Drawing a form in front of her and taking up her pen)* Perhaps we'd better start from the beginning. Name?

TRACEY Burgess.

GRIEVE First name?

TRACEY Tracey.

GRIEVE Address?

TRACEY D'you mean here or at home?

GRIEVE I mean your permanent address.

TRACEY Oh! It's eighteen, Holmlea Gardens -

GRIEVE How do you spell that?

TRACEY H O L M L E A G A -

GRIEVE *(Who knows how to spell 'Gardens')* Yes, that's all I needed.

TRACEY Oh, sorry - Pendwick, Lancs.

GRIEVE Postcode?

TRACEY Yes, but I don't know it.

GRIEVE And where are you staying in London?

TRACEY With a friend?

GRIEVE Oh, yes? And what's your friend's name and address?

TRACEY Charlene Mackley, 13c Brewers Alley, W C 2.

GRIEVE *(Very casually)* Ah! So your friend's a girl, then?

TRACEY *(Equally casually)* Yes. *(Then, suddenly offended, as the significance of the question dawns on her)* Yes, of course.

GRIEVE *(Showing no sign of noticing)* And how long have you been staying with her?

TRACEY A few weeks. Nearly a month.

GRIEVE Have you done any work while you've been there?

TRACEY I've helped a bit at the club.

GRIEVE *(Looking up, concealing a sudden suspicion)* Club?

TRACEY It's called Eve's Apple.

GRIEVE *(Poker-faced)* And where is it exactly?

TRACEY It's in Half-World Street. Soho, you know.

GRIEVE Number?

TRACEY Sixty-six. It's just opposite that big cinema that's showing *The Mark of the Beast.*

GRIEVE What were you doing there?

TRACEY Just helping out.

GRIEVE Did they pay you?

TRACEY Not yet. I'm still learning, you see.

GRIEVE *(Who sees only too well)* Yes, I think I do. What about your friend - do you pay her rent?

TRACEY Seventy pounds a week.

GRIEVE *(Who cannot completely conceal a startled look)* Really? Including food?

TRACEY *(Totally unaware that MRS GRIEVE thinks it anything out of the ordinary)* We don't eat there much, but we take it in turns to buy the coffee and stuff.

GRIEVE So what have you been living on?

TRACEY Cafes, mostly.

GRIEVE Yes, but where did you get the money for the cafes?

TRACEY I brought some with me.

GRIEVE And where's it gone?

TRACEY I've finished it.

GRIEVE Already? How much did you bring?

TRACEY *(Miserably)* A thousand pounds.

GRIEVE *(Thunderstruck)* A thousand pounds? And it's all gone in less than a month? What did you do with it?

TRACEY Well, there was seventy a week to Charlene, and meals are so expensive in London,and some of it I just spent -

GRIEVE *(Who can see that TRACEY is trying to hide something)* And the rest?

TRACEY *(Her defences collapsing)* I lost it.

GRIEVE Lost it? Where?

TRACEY At the club; at Eve's Apple.

GRIEVE How much money did you lose at the club?

TRACEY I'm not sure. I think it must have been about six hundred pounds.

GRIEVE What did you do then?

TRACEY *(In a very small voice)* Nothing.

GRIEVE Nothing? You lost six hundred pounds in a club where you were working without pay, and you did nothing about it? Didn't you tell the people in charge?

TRACEY *(Almost inaudible)* No.

GRIEVE Why not?

TRACEY Because Charlene might have lost her job.

GRIEVE Why? Did she take the money?

TRACEY *(Shocked)* Oh, no. But she thought they'd sack her. They don't like trouble at Eve's Apple.

GRIEVE How long ago did this happen?

TRACEY Two days.

GRIEVE Have you been to the police?

TRACEY No, I couldn't - because of Charlene.

GRIEVE So what are you going to do now?

TRACEY I've got to get some money. I've got nothing, so I can't even get a meal, and the rent's due.

GRIEVE The rent you pay Charlene?

TRACEY *(Cannot speak; she just nods)*

GRIEVE And whose idea was it that you came here?

TRACEY *(After several unsuccessful attempts to speak)* Charlene's.

GRIEVE *(Severely)* Was it? Well listen, my girl. Not one penny will you get out of me till you've reported this whole business to the police. Understand?

TRACEY But what about Charlene?

GRIEVE I'm afraid Charlene will have to manage her own affairs. You've just said yourself you've got nothing to eat, so it's that or starve.

She rings the bell on her desk. JENNIFER comes

in immediately and evinces a gleam of pleasure on seeing that TRACEY is almost in tears. This is not lost on MRS GRIEVE, who instantly feels more tender towards TRACEY.

JENNIFER You rang, Mrs Grieve?

GRIEVE *(To TRACEY)* Now, you run along and do the sensible thing. *(To JENNIFER)* Miss Burgess is ready to go now, Jennifer.

JENNIFER *(Looking stonily at TRACEY and jerking her head at the door)* This way.

TRACEY makes a wretched exit.

GRIEVE *(To JENNIFER)* There are some very foolish children about. *(With a sudden shudder of distaste at the whole sad story)* Don't send anyone in for a minute. I really must go and wash my hands.

MRS GRIEVE goes out through the private door of the office, while JENNIFER goes back to cow the applicants waiting in the hall.

END OF SCENE 4

SCENE 5

Half-World Street and Eve's Apple

HARRY steps out of the club and gazes up and down the road with the narrowed eyelids of the chancer perpetually on the make, when TRACEY comes trudging disconsolately along the street. Something about her manner alerts all his criminal instincts, and he sidles towards her in an exaggerated parody of friendliness that is charged with menace.

HARRY Hullo, little lady, and where might you be going?

TRACEY *(Frightened but defiant)* I'm going to the police.

Instantly Harry takes her arm in a grip like a handcuff, but his odiously friendly manner never falters.

HARRY Now why would you want to do a silly thing like that?

TRACEY Because of the money.

HARRY Money? What money?

TRACEY Six hundred pounds. I've lost it.

HARRY That's a nice little sum. Where did you lose it?

TRACEY At the club. At Eve's Apple.

HARRY *(Still smiling, but speaking through his teeth, as he drives his fingernails into her arm)* I fancy you must be mistaken about that, little lady. If you just think it over, I'm sure you'll remember that it was somewhere else.

TRACEY *(Terrified)* No, it was here. *(Her voice begins to rise towards a scream)* Stop that! You're hurting me.

Glancing hastily up and down the street, HARRY realises that violence is too risky and tries another tactic.

HARRY Well, even if you're right, there's no sense in telling the police and getting the club closed down. Don't kill the goose that lays the golden eggs, eh? Six hundred pounds isn't all that much. You could get much more than that through the club.

TRACEY *(Credulous as always)* Could I?

HARRY Of course you could. We've been keeping eye on you, little lady. You've got talent, and we've been waiting for the right moment to give you your chance.

TRACEY Really?

HARRY Yes, and - do you know? - I believe your time has come. Let's see if Rita's got a moment. *(Leading TRACEY gently into the club, he calls out)* Hey, Rita! Could you come and have a word with Tracey. I think she's just the one you're looking for.

Enter RITA

RITA What are you talking about, Harry?

HARRY I remember you saying, Rita, that you were looking for a nice young girl with talent, who could earn a lot of money. Well, poor Tracey has lost six hundred pounds, and she had some idea she might have mislaid it in the club. She was actually on her way to the police when I happened to mention to her that you had singled her out as our most talented newcomer. Isn't that right?

RITA *(Fixing TRACEY with a hypnotic smile)* It most certainly is, Tracey. I was saying to Harry only yesterday that I was sure I could find you some wonderful opportunities. Six hundred pounds! Why, you could earn that in two days, if you're a good girl and show what you're made of.

HARRY Rita, don't you think we ought to fix something for the poor girl straight away? After all, I expect she could do with the money, couldn't you, Tracey?

TRACEY *(Who cannot understand why she is feeling so nervous; after all, this is surely the opportunity she has been waiting for)* Thanks.

RITA All right, Harry. You take her up to the modelling room, and I'll see if I can't work something out for her. There's someone I'm thinking of - do you know who I mean?

HARRY I think I do.

RITA Well, I believe he could do a lot for Tracey if I put in a word for her. Run along, Tracey.

TRACEY *(Definitely alarmed)* Here, what's happening?

HARRY *(With a wolfish smile)* Come on, Tracey. This is your big chance.

He leads her out. RITA comes all the way downstage, possibly even through the audience and calls to Arthur in a shrill whisper.

ARTHUR is the man whom every woman fears, heavy, ugly and violent, devoid of tenderness or scruple. He is wearing a heavy coat with the collar turned up and a hat crushed down on his head. We never hear his voice or see more than his back, but the set of his neck on his broad shoulders tells us more than we want to know.

(If there is nobody willing or able to do justice to this part, the audience do not actually need to see ARTHUR at all. A skilful actress playing RITA can make an invisible ARTHUR more terrifying than any human being could hope to be.)

RITA *(Whispering, snake-like, with round eyes and a ghastly smile)* Arthur! You know what you were asking me the other day? Well, I know you can afford it, and I think I've found her for you. She's very young - just eighteen - and as innocent as a new-born babe. I've got her upstairs right now, so you'll have to hurry, but she'll be all ready for you when you get there. Only of course she doesn't know what's coming to her... So you will be gentle with her, won't you, Arthur? None of your rough stuff this time. Now I'm trusting you about that. Besides, she's a nice little thing. You'll be able to make a real pig of yourself with her.

Exit ARTHUR in the direction that HARRY and TRACEY went. RITA waits and listens with every sense a-quiver, when suddenly there is an offstage scream from TRACEY, a yell from HARRY, and TRACEY bursts onstage and dashes away, followed by HARRY, clutching his bruised shin.

RITA *(Continued)* Don't let her get away! Run after her!

HARRY How can I run after her? She nearly broke my leg.

RITA That's nothing to what Arthur will do, if we don't calm him down. Come on! Don't stand around here. Help me!

Exeunt RITA and HARRY back into Eve's Apple, and we see them no more.

END OF SCENE 5

SCENE 6

Back at the Department of Health and Social Security

As RITA and HARRY disappear into the bowels of the club, MRS GRIEVE returns to her desk and sits down to her papers. JENNIFER is just coming in to speak to her, when TRACEY, who has been running in a big circle (possibly right round the audience) bursts in and brushes past her.

JENNIFER *(furiously)* Here! You can't go in there.

TRACEY takes no notice of her but flings herself into the chair on MRS GRIEVE's right.

GRIEVE Goodness me! What is the - Oh! It's you!

TRACEY *(Howls through her tears)* I want to go home.

GRIEVE Did you go to the police? *(TRACEY, still sobbing, shakes her head)* Why not?

TRACEY Because - *(She tries to tell her, but finds she can't, so howls again)* I want to go home!

JENNIFER *(Beady-eyed)* Would you like to have her removed, Mrs Grieve? I could easily send for the porter.

GRIEVE No, thank you, Jennifer. I think I can manage, but I'll ring for you if I need you.

Recognising this for the snub it is, JENNIFER stamps out, thinking that, if she were in charge, things would be run very differently.

GRIEVE *(Continued, to TRACEY)* Now, something's happened, hasn't it? Are you going to tell me what it was?

TRACEY *(Tearstained, but beginning to grow calmer)* No, I can't. I just want to go home.

GRIEVE Yes, I know you do. And it's the most sensible thing I've heard you say since the first time you came into this office. Now do you know what this paper is?

TRACEY No.

GRIEVE It's a single, second-class railway warrant, and I'm putting in your name, Tracey Burgess, so that nobody can use it but you. And your home is in Pendwick, so I'll make it out to - ?

TRACEY Pendwick Junction *(and then, as an afterthought)* please.

GRIEVE Well, you'll want to go back to that flat and pack.

TRACEY No, I'm not going back there.

GRIEVE Oh dear! Well, let's have a look at the timetable... *(She does so)* Ah, there's a train in half an hour. Have you got your fare for the underground?

TRACEY *(Silently shakes her head)*

GRIEVE Hm! It's strictly against the Regulations, but let me see what I've got in my bag. There! I think a pound should be enough, and here's fifty pence for a cup of tea and a bun. *(She hands over the money)*

TRACEY *(Dazed, as she takes it)* Thanks. *(Then, coming to with a start)* Thanks a lot. You're sweet.

Impulsively, she leans over the desk and kisses MRS GRIEVE, just as JENNIFER comes into the room. Wondering if she has been disrespectful, TRACEY scuttles to the door and turns for a moment.

TRACEY *(Continued)* Thanks again. Goodbye.

Exit TRACEY, with JENNIFER looking daggers after her. Recollecting herself, she speaks to MRS GRIEVE.

JENNIFER Is it all right if I go for my tea now, Mrs Grieve? I'm five minutes late, as it is.

But MRS GRIEVES has never been kissed by an applicant before. The experience has made her feel pretty and almost young again. Her mind is in a pleasant dream, as she speaks kindly and vaguely to JENNIFER.

GRIEVE Of course, Jennifer dear; and don't hurry back. Take a nice long tea break. I really think I could do with one myself.

JENNIFER looks at MRS GRIEVE in surprise before going off into the outer office. MRS GRIEVE gives a little sigh of pleasure and goes into her inner sanctum.

END OF SCENE 6

SCENE 7:

Back at Holmlea Gardens

The kettle is boiling in the kitchen as MOTHER comes in to make a cup of tea. She calls to ELSIE, who is allegedly doing something in the next room.

MOTHER Elsie! I'm making a cup of tea. Will you have one before you go.

Enter ELSIE, taking off her overall, which she puts in her shopping bag.

ELSIE All right, Mrs Burgess, if you're having one yourself. *(plumping herself down comfortably in the centre chair)* I must say, I think I've earned it. The silver really looks a treat.

MOTHER Did you manage to do out the fridge?

ELSIE Well, not really. You can't do much with that fridge any more. I honestly think you'd be better with a new one.

MOTHER *(Sighing, as she sits in the chair on ELSIE's right)* Well, here's your tea, anyway.

ELSIE *(With deceptive carelessness)* Any news of your Tracey? She must be having a wonderful time in London. I'd love to see one of her letters.

MOTHER *(Evasively)* She's very busy, you know. Doesn't have much time for writing.

ELSIE They're all the same, aren't they? You can't get them to put pen to paper. Thank your stars for the telephone; that's what I say.

MOTHER Yes, but that's expensive.

ELSIE Don't I know it! Of course it shouldn't bother Tracey, with all the money she's got, but they never have the change for a box, do they? I bet she's ringing up every other day and reversing the charges.

MOTHER *(Unhappily)* No, not all that often.

ELSIE Still, the great thing is, you know she's in good hands. Who did you say she was staying with?

MOTHER A friend of hers from school, a girl called Charlene.

ELSIE *(Her eyes going round)* You don't mean Charlene Mackley?

MOTHER Yes, that's the name.

ELSIE Well, it's not for me to say anything. I mean, if that's the kind of girl you want Tracey to go around with...

MOTHER *(Unconvincingly)* I believe she's a very nice girl.

At this slightly uneasy moment, FATHER enters through the front door, coming home from work. His wife rises to meet him, and he kisses her before noticing ELSIE.

FATHER Evening, love. Any news from - Oh, hullo, Elsie.

ELSIE Evening, Mr Burgess. We were just talking about your young Tracey, and how she's getting on in London.

FATHER *(Defensively)* Oh... Yes... Do I see a cup of tea?

MOTHER I'll get you a cup and saucer.

ELSIE *(Not to be diverted)* Has she got a job yet?

FATHER *(Nonplussed)* Well, it takes a bit of time, you know. She's looking around and being a bit choosy.

He sits in the chair recently vacated by MOTHER.

ELSIE I'm off to my sister at Torquay next week.

FATHER *(With rather too obvious relief)* Oh, good! I mean, we shall miss you, but I'm sure you'll enjoy it there.

ELSIE Yes, it's beautiful country. I'll send you a postcard, of course. I'd like to send Tracey one, too. Could you give me her address?

FATHER I don't think she's got a really permanent address at present. She's staying with friends.

ELSIE Yes, Mrs Burgess was saying; Charlene Mackley, wasn't it?

FATHER *(Floundering)* Yes, er -

ELSIE All right. Give me Charlene's address. I can send it care of her.

FATHER *(Desperately)* I don't know that we ought to put Charlene to that trouble.

ELSIE Charlene won't mind. I remember her well. She didn't mind anything.

MOTHER *(Putting down his tea)* It's no good, love. She'll get it out of us soon or later. *(To ELSIE)* We don't know her address.

FATHER But we'd be grateful if that didn't go any further.

ELSIE Me? I'd never tell a soul.

MOTHER *(To FATHER)* I wish you'd never given her that money.

FATHER I didn't have any option. Anyway, we agreed to give it to her.

MOTHER Well, I don't know about that, but I shouldn't have listened to you. She's gone away to London, and we shall never see her again.

MOTHER breaks down in tears. FATHER is sitting in her chair, and so ELSIE, whose little strategy has worked better than she could have hoped, jumps up to offer sympathy.

ELSIE *(Offering her own chair)* There, there, Mrs Burgess. You sit down here. Have a good cry. It often helps.

FATHER's position is now in ruins. Not only is he responsible for TRACEY's disappearance, but he has even failed to offer his wife a chair in her moment of need. Too late to be of any help, he stands up and, finding himself useless, walks across the room and stares moodily out of the window.

MOTHER *(Crying bitterly)* It doesn't help at all. I don't want a good cry. I want my baby girl back.

ELSIE *(Triumphantly pursuing the last fleeing remnants of hope)* Don't you worry. Tracey's a sensible girl. She won't get into any trouble. Not like that Sally Hammond. I'm sure you heard about her.

MOTHER *(Looking up in horror through her tears)* No.

ELSIE *(With relish)* She went to London, all by herself, and she got in with a bad set. You know - drugs and all that. I think they call it Cannibal.

MOTHER *(Like a rabbit hypnotised by a snake)* What happened to her?

ELSIE I don't know. They never would say. But one thing's certain: She never came back to Pendwick.

MOTHER *(In a great upsurge of grief)* Oh my Tracey, my little girl, where are you now?

It is at this precise moment that TRACEY fits her latchkey in the keyhole and silently opens the door. MOTHER is too busy sobbing, and ELSIE too busy comforting her, for either of them to notice her. FATHER, in dumbstruck unbelief, watches her come in but cannot say a word. TRACEY stands before him like a dog expecting a whipping, but when nothing comes, she throws herself into his arms.

ELSIE *(Enjoying the scene hugely)* That's right, Mrs Burgess. Don't try to control yourself. It'll relieve your feelings.

Slowly revolving with TRACEY in his arms, FATHER tries to attract their attention but without success.

MOTHER I would give anything to have her back, just as she was, five weeks ago.

ELSIE I know, but we can't bring back the past. It's all water under the bridge.

FATHER Look, love -

MOTHER *(Stalwartly refusing to look at him)* Don't you try to get round me. Haven't you done enough?

FATHER But it's Tracey!

MOTHER *(Almost hysterically)* Yes, of course it's Tracey. Who do you think I've been worrying about all these weeks. I can't get her out of my mind. All the time, it's just as if she was standing there before my...

In saying this, she has swung round to face her husband, so that TRACEY has suddenly come into her field of vision. Her voice trails away, and she and ELSIE can only stare dumbly at the vision.

TRACEY *(Finding her voice at last)* Mum, I'm sorry.

MOTHER *(Rising like a missile and gathering TRACEY in her arms)* Tracey! Oh, you naughty girl, where have you been?

FATHER *(Who knows a good sign when he sees one)* Well, she's back now, anyway.

ELSIE Yes, isn't that a surprise! I'm so glad for you. *(From the tone of her voice, she doesn't sound very glad on her own account)*

MOTHER *(Turning to ELSIE with a new coldness in her voice)* I expect you'll be wanting to get along now, Elsie. Have a nice time in Torquay.

ELSIE *(Bridling)* Yes, of course, Mrs Burgess. I expect you'll have things to say to Tracey that you wouldn't like other people to hear. I'll just get my coat.

ELSIE goes off to fetch her coat.

TRACEY *(In a small voice)* I knew you were going to be cross.

MOTHER Cross? Of course I'm not cross, you daft little creature. I'm just so relieved. Oh, why didn't you write? Why didn't you 'phone?

TRACEY I don't know. I just couldn't.

FATHER You didn't get a job, then?

TRACEY No.

FATHER And the money?

TRACEY It's gone. And Mum's blue suitcase. I'm so sorry. I thought perhaps I could do the cleaning for you - instead of Elsie. It might save you a bit of money.

ELSIE has come in and heard this suggestion

ELSIE *(Furious)* Oh, charming! Well I'd better be off.

MOTHER Don't be silly, Tracey. We don't want you to do the cleaning. We're just so thrilled to have you back.

FATHER I tell you what: Why don't we all go out for a celebration supper at the King's Head?

MOTHER *(Taking light)* That's a lovely idea.

FATHER You go and put on something pretty, while I ring up and book a table.

At this moment, ELSIE reaches the front door, just as KATHRYN opens it with her latchkey, but the other three are too excited to notice.

KATHRYN *(To ELSIE, in indignant surprise)* What's all this?

ELSIE *(Vengefully)* Oh, Kathryn, isn't it lovely! Your little sister's come back, and they're going to take her out to supper as a special treat.

Satisfied that she cannot improve on this final thrust, ELSIE passes out into the street.

KATHRYN *(After watching in silence while the other three cuddle each other)* Good evening!

FATHER *(Not the world's most sensitive man)* Hullo, Kathryn. Look who's back!

KATHRYN *(With a face like a rat-trap)* Yes, I can see.

MOTHER *(Smelling trouble)* Your father's taking us all out to dinner, love, at the King's Head.

KATHRYN Oh, good! I hope you have a nice time.

MOTHER But you're coming too?

KATHRYN No, I don't think so, thank you. I've got to go out.

KATHRYN turns round and walks straight out of the front door again, slamming it behind her. Then she makes her way grimly down towards the audience.

MOTHER *(Horrified, to FATHER)* Go after her, love! Quick, stop her! You can't let her go like that.

Bewildered but obedient, FATHER stumbles out of the house after KATHRYN.

FATHER *(Calling)* Kathryn! Kathryn, stop a moment!

KATHRYN stops in her tracks but does not turn round. He catches up with her.

FATHER *(Continuing in a lower voice)* Kathryn, please come back into the house. Is there something the matter?

KATHRYN *(As before)* No. Everything's fine.

FATHER There is something, isn't there, Kathryn? Please tell me.

KATHRYN Don't you know?

FATHER No, I don't.

KATHRYN For five years now I've been going out to work, making my bed every morning, keeping my room tidy, paying in money for the housekeeping every week, and when did you even take me to the pizza house? Then Tracey goes away for a month and you never hear a word or a line from her, and now you're taking her out to the King's Head!

FATHER *(Still puzzled)* But you're coming too.

KATHRYN *(Giving it up)* Oh, Dad, you'll never understand.

FATHER *(As the light dawns)* Yes, I do see what you mean. *(Rather clumsily, he puts his arms round KATHRYN)* Look, love: You've been a wonderful daughter to your mum and me, and we both know it. You were the only comfort we had while Tracey was away, and we shall never forget how good you've been. We got a bit excited tonight, with Tracey coming home, so please make allowances for us.

For the first time for years, KATHRYN is crying in her FATHER's arms.

KATHRYN *(Through her sobs)* You're always cuddling her, and you never touch me.

FATHER Please come to the King's Head, Kathryn. It wouldn't be the same without you.

He directs a vague kiss somewhere into her hair and leads her gently back into the house. TRACEY runs to her and kisses her.

TRACEY Kathy, I'm so sorry.

KATHRYN It's all right, Tracey. I'm coming.

MOTHER, who feels as if she has been holding

her breath for the last two minutes, lets out a long sigh of relief.

FATHER: *(With a sudden rush of energy)* Well, we'd better hurry, or they may not have a table. You all go and get changed while I ring the King's Head.

TRACEY *(Giggling)* Aren't you going to change, Dad?

FATHER Yes, why not? I think I might put on my Christmas tie.

For some reason we shall never know, this strikes them all as funny. The two girls rush off towards the stairs, with MOTHER following them, while FATHER goes into the next room, muttering to himself.

FATHER *(Continued, muttering to himself)* Now, I wonder where Elsie's put the phone book this time.

He disappears into the next room.

THE END